GET ACTIVE!

WINTER SPORTS

Barbara C. Bourassa

First published in the United States by
QEB Publishing, Inc.
23062 La Cadena Drive
Laguna Hills, CA 92653

www.qeb-publishing.com

Library of Congress Control Number: 2007000932

ISBN 978-1-59566-348-1

Written by Barbara C. Bourassa
Edited, designed, and picture researched by
   Starry Dog Books Ltd
Consultant Steven Downes, of the Sports Journalists'
   Association www.sportsjournalists.co.uk

Publisher Steve Evans
Creative Director Zeta Davies
Senior Editor Hannah Ray

Printed and bound in China

Web site information is correct at time of going to press. However, the publishers cannot accept liability for any information or links found on third-party Web sites.

All the sports in this book involve varying degrees of difficulty and the publisher would strongly advise that none of the activities mentioned is undertaken without adult supervision or the guidance of a professional coach.

CURR
GV
841.15
.B6r
2007

Words in **bold** can be found in the Glossary on pages 30–31.

Picture credits
Key: t=top, b=bottom, l=left, r=right, c=center, FC = front cover, BC = back cover

S = Shutterstock.com, C = Corbis, D = Dreamstime.com, G = Getty Images, BSP = Big Stock Photo.com, ISP = iStockphoto.com, F = Fotolia.com

FC (main image) C/ © David Stoecklein, (top to bottom) ISP/ © Andrei Tchernov, S/ © Kondrachov Vladimir, S/ © C.Paquin, ISP/ © Bill Grove, ISP/ © Jason Lugo, S/ © Melissa King, S/ © Irina Terentjeva. BC S/ © Joy Strotz.1 S/ © Irina Terentjeva; 4 S/ © PhotoCreate; 5l S/ © Matt Baker, 5r (top to bottom) S/ © C. Paquin, ISP/ © Dieter Hawlan, S/ © Svetlana Larina, ISP/ © Bill Grove; 6t S/ © Maxim Petrichuk, 6b ISP/ © Anna Chelnokova; 7 (main image) G/ © Lori Adamski Peek, 7bl C/ © Tim De Waele/Isosport; 8t BSP/ © Freddy, 8b S/ © Action Photos; 9 G/ © Mike Powell; 10b C/ © Steven G. Smith; 11 C/ © Mike Chew; 12bl C/ © Reuters, 12br S/ © JJJ; 12–13 C/ © Arno Balzarini/epa; 13t ISP/ © Sandramo; 14t F/ © ximagination, 14b G © David Handley; 15 C/ © Richard Hamilton Smith; 16t C/ © Bartomiej Zborowski/ epa, 16b S/ © Karina Maybely Orellana Rojas; 17 C/ © David Brooks; 18t ISP/ © Miha Urbanija, 18b S/ © C.Paquin; 19 G/ © Christopher Thomas; 20t S/ © Robert Fullerton, 20b C/ © Andreas Meier/Reuters; 21 C/ © Fabrizio Bensch/ Reuters; 22t D/ © Simonkr, 22–23 C/ © Don Mason; 23t C/ © Don Mason; 24t Joy Green, courtesy skijornow. com, 24b C/ © Galen Rowell; 25t S/ © Pierdelune, 25 (main image) C/ © Alessia Pierdomenico/Reuters; 26t C/ © Matthias Schrader/epa, 26b G/ © Glyn Kirk; 27 C/ © David Stoecklein; 28t S/ © Pyastolova Nadya, 28b S/ © Dvoretskiy Igor Vladimirovich; 29 courtesy of www. snow-valley.com; 31 S/ © Nick Stubbs.

CONTENTS

INTRODUCTION

THE winter sports that are grouped together in this book are usually done in places where there is plenty of snow and ice. Some can be done all year round, such as ice skating (in an indoor **rink**) or downhill skiing (on **artificial snow**), but for the most part, the sports are meant to be done outside. Many of them began in countries that are snowy for many months of the year.

The first snowboard, called the snurfer, was developed in the 1960s. The idea came from joining two skis together.

Snow time!
Some winter sports, such as snowboarding and downhill skiing, are especially fun to do just after a heavy snowfall! Skating and ice hockey, of course, require ice. And cross-country skiing and snowmobiling can be done on just a few inches of snow.

REMEMBER TO TAKE IT SLOWLY!

Before you take up any new sport, it is important to remember that the **professionals** you see performing on television—for instance, ski jumping or playing ice hockey—are very experienced and most of them have been practicing for years. So don't expect to be able to do the same moves or go as fast as they do, without first learning the basics of your chosen sport.

Safety first

You'll notice that most children wear helmets when snowboarding, downhill skiing, or playing ice hockey.

Helmets provide protection for the head if you fall. Ice hockey also requires lots of body padding for protection against flying **pucks**, raised sticks, and other players! Different sports need different gear, and wearing the right protective gear for your winter sport will help keep you safe while having fun!

Coaching tips

As any good **coach** will tell you, learning a new sport means understanding and mastering the basic skills, taking good care of your equipment, and practicing a lot. All winter sports, from sledding to ski jumping, are part of a healthy and active lifestyle. Remember to drink plenty of water, eat well, and take breaks whenever you need to, whether you're playing ice hockey or cross-country skiing along wooded **trails**.

SNOWBOARDING

SNOWBOARDING is a relatively new sport. It involves riding a special board down a snow-covered hill or mountain. Since becoming an Olympic sport, snowboarding has become much more popular.

Riding the board

A snowboard is larger than a **skateboard**, but smaller than a **surfboard**. To ride the board, you stand on it sideways wearing snowboard boots, which fit into **bindings** that hold the boots to the board. Snowboarders wear all the usual warm winter gear—snow pants, warm coat, gloves—and often goggles to protect their eyes from the glare of the sun.

If you are just learning to snowboard, holding your arms out to the sides will help you balance.

REACHING THE TOP

To get up big hills, such as those found at snowboard or ski resorts, snowboarders use a lift. On some, you stand on your board while the lift pulls you up the hill. On others, you sit in a chair (a chairlift, above) or ride in a gondola (an enclosed cabin) and are carried up the hill.

Sense of balance

Snowboarding requires good balance. You need to be able to shift your weight to stay upright as you move along, especially when moving fast. When you first learn to snowboard, you'll probably fall down a lot—this is normal! But you will get the hang of it quickly. To learn more about snowboarding, check out this Web site:
www.abc-of-snowboarding.com

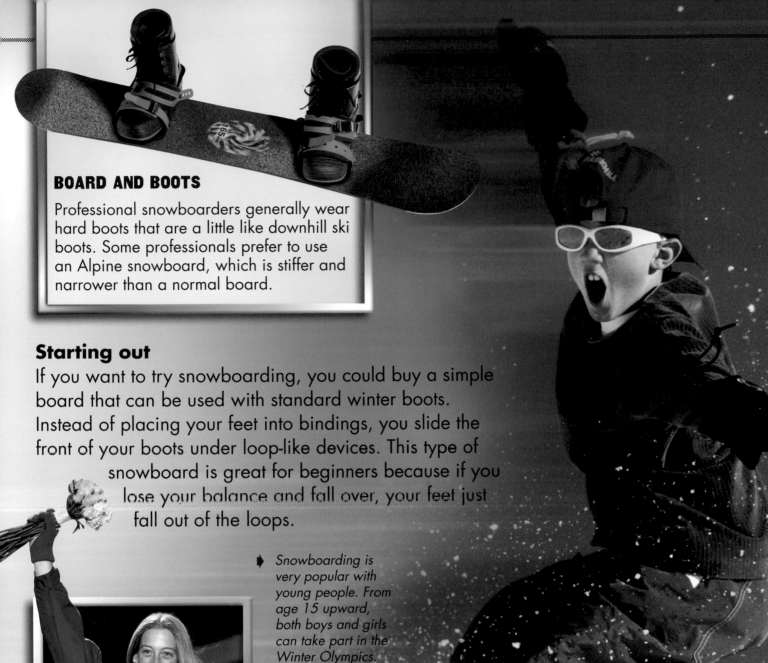

BOARD AND BOOTS

Professional snowboarders generally wear hard boots that are a little like downhill ski boots. Some professionals prefer to use an Alpine snowboard, which is stiffer and narrower than a normal board.

Starting out

If you want to try snowboarding, you could buy a simple board that can be used with standard winter boots. Instead of placing your feet into bindings, you slide the front of your boots under loop-like devices. This type of snowboard is great for beginners because if you lose your balance and fall over, your feet just fall out of the loops.

▶ *Snowboarding is very popular with young people. From age 15 upward, both boys and girls can take part in the Winter Olympics.*

WORLD RECORD

According to the Guinness Book of World Records, Karine Ruby of France has won a record 11 women's World Cup snowboarding titles.

Where to snowboard

Anywhere that's suitable for skiing or sledding is also suitable for snowboarding. But be sure to watch out for other people and trees that might be in your path! More advanced snowboarders can visit a snowboard park (also called a terrain park). Some terrain parks are stand-alone, meaning they are only designed for snowboarders. Others are part of a larger resort that has separate areas for downhill skiers and snowboarders on the same mountain.

Terrain park obstacles

Terrain parks have small hills that snowboarders ride or jump over. These parks also have rails, which snowboarders slide down. In an event called snowboard cross, snowboarders race down a course. The fastest snowboarder wins!

➥ *To slide down a terrain park rail, you need to have excellent balance and plenty of experience.*

SNOWBOARD LINGO

Snowboarding has a language all its own. The terms vary depending on where you're snowboarding. In the USA, to "roll down the windows" means to swing your arms wildly in the air in an attempt to catch your balance. "Huckers" are snowboarders who fling themselves through the air, but do not land on their feet.

International champions

At the 2006 Winter Olympics in Turin, Italy, many of the medal-winning snowboarders came from snowy countries. They included Philip Schoch of Sweden, Paul-Henri Delerue of France, Amelie Kober of Germany, and Dominique Maltais of Canada.

SNOWBOARD SAFETY

If you are just learning to snowboard, don't be tempted to go down steep hills or over jumps too soon. It is far better to start slowly and learn the sport carefully than to end up with an injury.

Half pipe

Professional snowboarders compete in various kinds of competitions. One takes place on a feature called a half-pipe—a long, smooth channel in the snow. It looks like a tube that's been cut in half lengthways. In the men's and women's half-pipe event, experienced snowboarders perform jumps, flips, and other moves along the edge of the half-pipe or inside it.

HISTORY OF SNOWBOARDING

Snowboarding has only been around for about 50 years. It could have been started by a skateboarder who took off his wheels, or a surfer who used a **boogie board** in winter. But it most likely started with someone binding two skis together.

The Alley Oop trick is only for the most experienced snowboarders. It involves doing a 180-degree turn in midair above the lip, or top edge, of the half-pipe.

DOWNHILL SKIING

DOWNHILL skiing (also called Alpine skiing) is a fun sport. The aim is to ride your skis downhill, making turns, going over small bumps, and feeling the wind in your face. When you ski, you balance yourself on two skis. You need to keep your skis next to each other and pointing in the right direction. This can take some practice, so don't be surprised if you fall over a few times!

EQUIPMENT

To try downhill skiing, you'll need a pair of skis and ski boots, which attach to the skis with metal bindings. It's also helpful to have poles to help push yourself along or steer your way downhill. For warmth and safety, it's best to wear a warm ski jacket and pants, a hat, gloves, a helmet, and eye protection, such as goggles or sunglasses.

◄ *For young skiers, like this three-year-old, a moving carpet is a great way to be carried up a small hill.*

Going up!

If you are skiing at a ski resort, you will probably take a lift up the mountain. On some lifts, you keep your skis on and the lift pulls or carries you up the hill. If you ride in a gondola (an enclosed cabin) you take your skis off and sit or stand for the ride up the mountain. Some ski resorts have a "moving carpet"—a large, flat **conveyor belt** that carries you up a slope with your skis on. At the top, you step off the moving carpet and ski back down the hill.

Gentle slopes

If you are a beginner, you will probably learn to ski on a small hill (called a bunny hill), where you can get used to the feeling of wearing ski boots and moving around on skis. As you progress, you can move to a steeper hill or **trail**.

DID YOU KNOW?

Mountain ranges all over the world have been used for downhill skiing. Among the most famous are the Swiss Alps (in Switzerland), where you can find ski resorts such as Davos, St. Moritz, and Wengen. There are other famous ski resorts in the Andes— the long mountain range that runs down the west coast of South America—as well as in the USA and Canada.

▲ Most skiers wear sunglasses to protect their eyes from the sun reflecting off the snow, or goggles to protect their eyes against wind and snow.

Olympic events

Downhill skiing is fun to do, and it's also very exciting to watch! The Winter Olympics feature a number of different events that involve downhill skiing. Some are races in which skiers ski down a mountain as fast as they can. In other events, skiers are judged on their ability to ski over bumps (called **moguls**) or perform difficult maneuvers (freestyle).

Races

There are many different kinds of downhill ski races. In a **slalom** race, skiers race downhill making tight turns around a set of skinny, flexible poles called slalom poles. The poles are stuck in the snow along the track. The skier who skis down the course the fastest, without missing any poles, wins the race. Slalom racers wear special padding on their legs and arms in case they hit the poles as they fly by.

Freestyle

In a freestyle, or **aerial**, skiing event, a skier skis down a ramp that sends him or her up into the air. The skier then has three or four seconds to perform tricks, such as flips, twists, and spirals. Judges watch how well the skier lands and determine the difficulty of the maneuvers performed in the air.

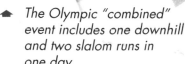

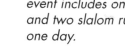

▲ The Olympic "combined" event includes one downhill and two slalom runs in one day.

SKI RESCUE

If a skier at a resort falls and gets hurt, he or she may be rescued by the ski patrol. These experienced skiers ski around all day looking for people who need help. Sometimes helicopters are used to rescue skiers from the highest mountains.

Downhill

In an event called the downhill, skiers race one at a time down a steep, winding course as fast as they can. The skier who gets to the bottom the fastest is the winner. Downhill racers wear padded ski outfits. Skiers' outfits fit close to their bodies in order to make them more **aerodynamic**. The pads, as well as their helmets, protect them in case they fall.

▲ Tina Maze of Slovakia speeds downhill during an Alpine Ski World Cup Women's Super-G race in St. Moritz, Switzerland (January 2006). Maze finished in second place.

SKATING is a fun sport in which you wear ice skates—boots with sharp blades on the bottom—to move quickly across ice. People skate on frozen ponds and lakes in winter or on indoor or outdoor skating rinks. Some people skate just for fun! Others master all kinds of difficult maneuvers that they perform in front of judges in skating competitions.

SKATE FACTS

Skaters can choose different types of skates depending on their skill or the kind of skating they want to do. (Check out www.isu.org for information about different kinds of skating.) Beginners wear basic recreational skates, while professional skaters wear skates specially made to fit their feet.

Figure skating

In **figure skating** competitions, skaters perform twirls, flips, and jumps, usually to music. Figure skaters at the Winter Olympics are judged on how well they perform their maneuvers, how difficult the moves are, and how well they skate with their partners. There are singles competitions for solo men and women skaters, pairs skating, and ice dancing.

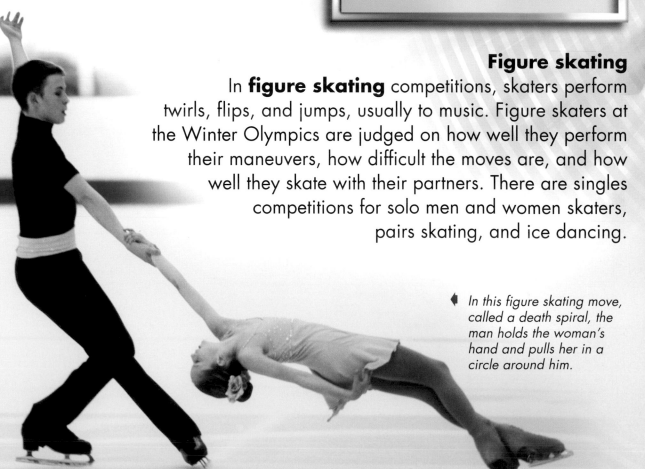

◀ In this figure skating move, called a death spiral, the man holds the woman's hand and pulls her in a circle around him.

Balancing act

Skating requires good balance—after all, you need to support the weight of your entire body on two very thin pieces of metal. If you are a beginner, you should expect to fall down a lot! Also, you may get sore ankles because they have to work hard to keep your feet at the right angles.

◄ *These kids are having a friendly speed-skating race. Speed skating is also an exciting Winter Olympic sport, in which skaters race around an oval-shaped rink.*

DID YOU KNOW?

The machine that cleans the ice at a skating rink is called a Zamboni. It is named for Frank Zamboni, its inventor.

15

ICE HOCKEY

ONCE YOU know how to skate, you may want to learn how to play ice hockey. Ice hockey is a fast-paced, exciting game played on ice with sticks and a puck. A puck is a hard, smooth disc that glides easily across the ice. The aim is to hit the puck into the goal more often than the other team. The team with the most goals wins.

The stick

The bottom part of a hockey stick is called the blade. The blade is used to push the puck along the ice. Some ice hockey players wrap tape around the ends of their sticks to give them better grip on the puck.

OLYMPIC RIVALS

Ice hockey is a popular Winter Olympic sport. Rivalry between Finland, the USA, Russia (above, in red, playing Slovakia), and Norway is legendary. At the 2006 Winter Olympics, Sweden won the men's gold medal, while Canada won the women's event.

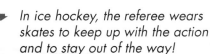

➦ In ice hockey, the referee wears skates to keep up with the action and to stay out of the way!

Game basics

There may be up to 22 players on an ice hockey team, but only six play at one time. One of them is the goalkeeper, two play **defense**, and three are **forwards**. The action is so fast-paced that players are substituted every few minutes. Hockey is played on a rink. The rink is marked with colored lines painted beneath the ice.

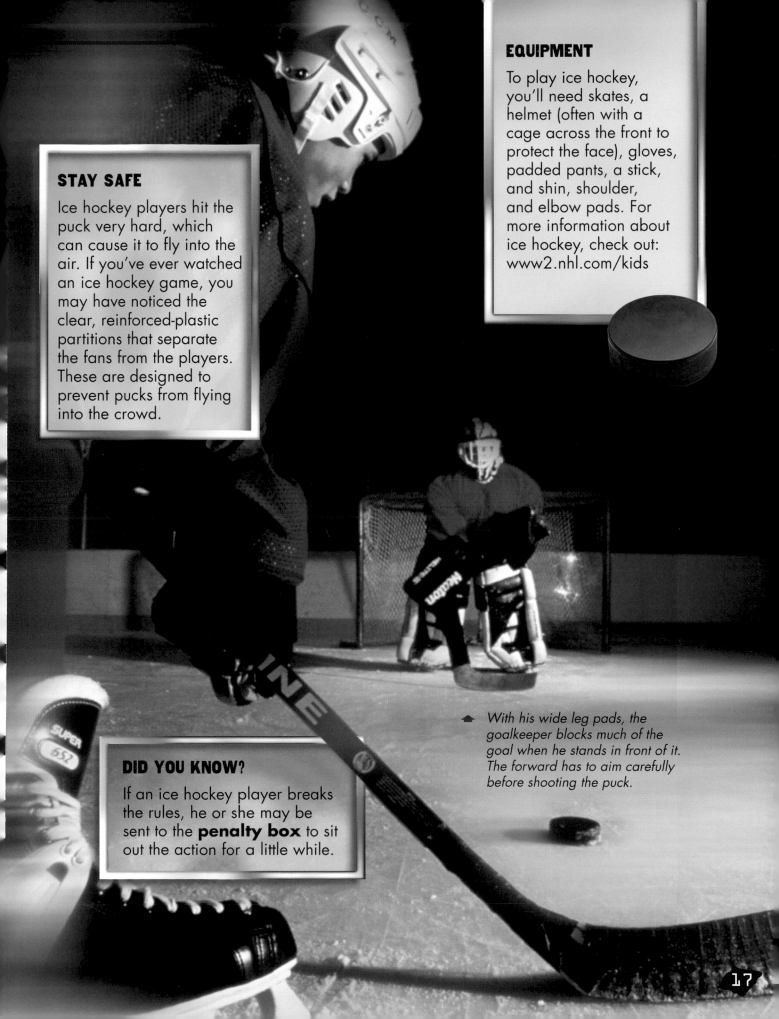

STAY SAFE

Ice hockey players hit the puck very hard, which can cause it to fly into the air. If you've ever watched an ice hockey game, you may have noticed the clear, reinforced-plastic partitions that separate the fans from the players. These are designed to prevent pucks from flying into the crowd.

EQUIPMENT

To play ice hockey, you'll need skates, a helmet (often with a cage across the front to protect the face), gloves, padded pants, a stick, and shin, shoulder, and elbow pads. For more information about ice hockey, check out: www2.nhl.com/kids

DID YOU KNOW?

If an ice hockey player breaks the rules, he or she may be sent to the **penalty box** to sit out the action for a little while.

With his wide leg pads, the goalkeeper blocks much of the goal when he stands in front of it. The forward has to aim carefully before shooting the puck.

SLEDDING

SLEDDING is probably the easiest winter sport to try—all you need is a snow-covered hill and a sled of some kind.

Sled types
Sleds come in many shapes and sizes. On an old-fashioned toboggan, several people can sit together, one behind the other. A flying saucer, on the other hand, is meant for just one person. It resembles cartoon drawings of **UFO**s from outer space!

DOG SLED RACE
In Alaska, sleds pulled by teams of dogs compete in the Iditarod Trail **Sled** Dog Race. Competitors in this annual race travel more than 1,000 miles (1,609km) over snow and ice.

Look out below!
The first place you are likely to try sledding is in your yard (if it has a hill) or in a park. The hill doesn't have to be big. It's important that you can see the bottom of the hill from the top, so you don't bump into anything on the way down. (You'll need to ask permission if you want to sled on someone else's property.)

◆ Many modern sleds, like this flying saucer, are made of plastic and have handles to hold onto.

Staying warm

You'll need to dress warm for sledding: thick pants, a coat, mittens or gloves, and a hat (or helmet). Don't forget to take a thermos full of hot chocolate to warm you up and a snack to give you energy to walk back up the hill.

SLEDDING WITHOUT SNOW

Just because some people live in parts of the world where there isn't much snow, doesn't mean they can't enjoy sledding! On the islands of Hawaii, children ride banana tree stumps down grassy hills. For an extreme version of sledding, the ancient Hawaiians rode wooden sleds down hills of hardened **lava**.

This toboggan has two runners with a raised seat in between. The person in front holds onto the sled, and the person in back holds onto the person in front.

SLEDDING EVENTS

IF YOU LIKE sledding, you may also like watching sports that involve sleds. At the Winter Olympics there are several events in which athletes ride a sledlike device down a hill, usually at very high speeds. The sleds have some unusual names: there's the two- or four-person **bobsled**, the **luge**, and the **skeleton**.

Fearless and fast

In the skeleton event, one person lies on a small sled and rides head first down an ice track. The aim is to reach the bottom in a faster time than the other competitors. In the luge competition, one or two riders lie on their backs on the luge and speed down the track feet first. The riders grip handles on the edge of the luge, which helps them steer.

▶ *Maya Pederson of Switzerland speeds down the track during her first run at the 2006 Skeleton World Cup in Switzerland.*

SNOW TUBING

If you are attracted to the idea of bobsledding, a good place to start might be with a very fast form of sledding called snow tubing. A snow tube is an inflated rubber ring that you sit on. The air provides a cushion between you and the ground, so the ride doesn't feel too bumpy! The tube moves fast because it's very light.

WHAT TO WEAR

All bobsled, luge, and skeleton athletes wear helmets to protect their heads and faces. They also wear tight racing suits to make their bodies more aerodynamic.

At the start of a four-man bobsled race, the teammates reach a speed of about 25 mph (40kph) before they jump on board.

Bobsledding

In the bobsled event, two or four riders sit one behind the other in a special sled. At the start of the race, the teammates push the bobsled to get it moving and then leap on and sit down. The bobsled races down a narrow, twisting ice track. Tracks are usually about 1,312 to 1,531 yards (1,200 to 1,400m) long. The bobsled reaches speeds of up to 81 mph (130kph). The team that makes it to the bottom in the fastest time wins!

CROSS-COUNTRY SKIING

CROSS-COUNTRY skiing is just what it sounds like: wearing a pair of skis to travel across country (rather than down a hill). You use two poles to stay balanced and to help push yourself along. Trails or tracks for cross-country skiers may wind through woods and across frozen lakes and fields. Classic-style cross-country skiing is a hobby sport, while professional skiers compete in races.

Classic style

The classic style of cross-country skiing is the easiest to learn. You place your skis side by side, about 6 inches (15cm) apart. Then slide one foot forward at a time, as if you were walking without taking your feet off the ground. Gradually the walking action will turn into skiing.

WHERE TO SKI

In some parts of the world, such as the USA, Canada, and northern Europe, you can ski on special trails—wide, flat areas of snow that have been prepared for easy skiing. Some people prefer to make their own trail, making a path across the countryside (above), and then spend the night in a tent. Brrr! Don't forget to ask permission if you want to ski across someone else's property.

Good exercise

Cross-country skiing is very good exercise because it uses many of the big **muscles** in your body, including your arms and legs. Most cross-country skiers don't wear bulky winter gear, but instead wrap up in layers of warm clothing that can be removed (or put back on) as the body heats up (or cools down).

When you are cross-country skiing, you use poles to provide balance and to prevent a fall.

SKIS

For cross-country skiing you will need a pair of cross-country skis—which are very long and narrow—a pair of boots and some poles. The boots are attached to the skis, but generally only at the toes. You lift your heels as you move along.

DID YOU KNOW?

In Finland, during the **Winter War** of 1939, some of the Finnish army wore cross-country skis while fighting the Russians.

Many people cross-country ski along paths that are used for hiking in the summer. If you are planning a long ski trip, bring food and drink to help give you energy.

CROSS-COUNTRY SKIING CONTINUED **2**

Racing for professionals

At the professional level, there are several types of cross-country ski races. In some events, skiers use the classic style of skiing; in others they "skate" along the snow (moving their skis from side to side in order to go faster).

The biathlon race

Cross-country skiing may date back to prehistoric times, when some people wore skis to hunt animals. This may explain the winter sport of biathlon, which combines cross-country skiing with rifle shooting. Competitors stop at a shooting range two or four times during the race. There, they fire a round of shots. The aim is to hit five targets with five bullets. There are various penalties for missing the targets.

DID YOU KNOW?

Skijoring is a sport that combines cross-country skiing with dogs (or sometimes horses). The skier is pulled along by the dogs.

Junior races

In northern Europe and Canada, children compete in the same types of cross-country ski races as adults. In a sprint-style race, you ski as fast as you can from one point to another. In a pursuit race, you start out doing one style of skiing (such as classic—sliding one foot forward and then the other), then stop halfway through the race, change to a second set of skis, and finish the race using the freestyle, or skating, style of cross-country skiing.

◄ Competitors in cross-country ski races, like these children in Oslo, Norway, wear numbered bibs so the judges know who's who.

Long-distance and relay races

Sweden has a race called the Vasaloppet, in which athletes ski for 56 miles (90km). It is considered by some to be the longest, oldest, and largest cross-country ski race in the world. In contrast, in ski relay races, four skiers in a team each ski a distance of 6.2 miles (10km) for men and 3.1 miles (5km) for women. The team that completes the course first wins!

▶ A competitor in a women's relay race at the cross-country skiing World Cup. In a relay, skiers take turns on the course.

SKI JUMPING

SKI JUMPING is a sport performed in competitions by highly experienced athletes. The skier skis down a long, steep slope with bent knees and his or her body close to the skis. This helps build up speed. From a ramp at the bottom, he or she launches into the air and leans forward so the body is almost parallel with the skis. After sailing through the air, the skier lands at the bottom of the hill. Points are scored for distance, and extra points are given for style and form. The ski jumper with the most points wins.

SKI JUMPING EQUIPMENT

The skis used in ski jumping are longer and wider than those used in downhill or cross-country skiing. The shape of the skis helps the jumper sail through the air. Professional ski jumpers wear helmets and close-fitting suits.

Three styles

At the professional level, there are three ski jumping events: normal hill, large hill, and team events. The best ski jumpers reach distances of 110 yards (100m) off the normal hill, and can fly through the air for 142 yards (130m) off the large hill.

➡ *From the top of this hill, the ski jumper can see the ramp at the bottom and the ski resort in Lillehammer, Norway, in the distance.*

OLYMPIC GOLD!

At the 2006 Winter Olympics, Lars Bystoel of Norway won gold in the normal hill competition. In the final round, Lars jumped an amazing 113 yards (103.5m).

Start small!

Ski jumping is a great sport to watch live or on televison. However, if you want to try it, first you need to learn how to downhill ski. Then learn how to do small jumps. Gradually, with lots of practice and the help of a coach, you can build up to doing bigger jumps.

◆ *Practicing jumps on small hills is a good way to get the feel of flying through the air.*

CANADIAN CHAMPION

Fourteen-year-old Trevor Morrice of Canada won the 2006 North American Junior Ski Jumping Championships. Trevor finished with 246.5 points on the K90 hill. The term K90 refers to the distance between where the skier leaves the jump (the takeoff) and the part of the hill where it starts to flatten out (called the **K point**). On a normal hill the distance is 98 yards, which is 90m—hence the name K90.

SNOWMOBILING

A SNOWMOBILE is a motorized sled powered by a gas engine. It has one central, **caterpillar track** and skis instead of wheels. To drive it, you sit on the back like you would on a motorcycle. Snowmobile racing is very popular. People race snowmobiles downhill, across country, and around ice tracks.

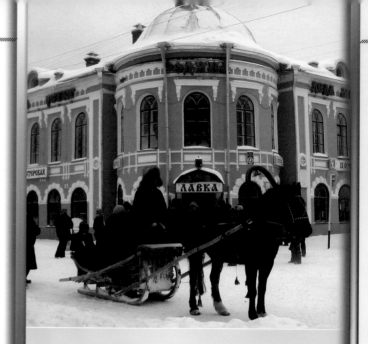

SLEIGH RIDING

Before the snowmobile was invented, people in snowy places often traveled by horse-drawn sleigh. Today, sleigh riding is a popular tourist activity in ski resorts and towns in snowy countries, such as Russia.

Iron Dog

The longest snowmobile race in the world takes place in Alaska and is called the Iron Dog. Competitors race a distance of more than 1,971 miles (3,172km).

Snow cats

Snow cats are large snow vehicles used for "grooming" ski trails. Running on caterpillar tracks, they pull along a bar-shaped device that flattens or smooths out the snow.

Some snow cats are used on ski mountains, some are used to transport people or goods in snowy parts of the world, and others are used to explore the **Arctic** region.

Be careful!

If you want to try snowmobiling, you'll need warm-weather gear—thick pants, a warm coat, gloves, and boots—as well as a helmet. Some snowmobiles are designed for two people—the passenger sits behind the driver and holds onto two side handles. Snowmobiles can go very fast, but unless you are experienced, it's best to keep your speed low and to always have adult supervision.

◀ *Snowmobiling is best in good weather conditions, when you can clearly see the trail ahead of you.*

SURVIVING THE WINTER

In some parts of the world, such as in the Arctic, snowmobiles and snow cats are an important means of transportation. Many people depend on them for survival, especially during the long winter months when thick snow covers the land.

aerial A style of downhill skiing in which skiers perform jumps, flips, twists, and other moves.

aerodynamic Something with a streamlined shape that allows wind or air to flow over it easily, making it go faster.

Arctic The icy region around the North Pole.

artificial snow Snow made by a machine.

bindings Devices that hold boots to skis or a snowboard. Downhill skiers insert their boots toe-first into the bindings, then put their heels down to snap the bindings closed around the boots. Snowboarders place their whole boots into the bindings, which have straps over the toes and ankles that they tighten by hand.

bobsled A long fiberglass or metal sled with two sets of steel runners. Bobsleds are big enough for two or four athletes to sit inside.

boogie board A smaller, shorter version of a surfboard ridden in shallow water.

caterpillar track A steel band looped around the wheels of a vehicle such as a snow cat. It allows the vehicle to travel over rough ground or across snow and ice.

coach An instructor or trainer who helps players improve their skills.

conveyor belt A continuous moving band that moves things from one place to another.

defense Players who defend their own goal and try to stop the other team from scoring.

figure skating Performing moves such as jumps or spins on ice, either alone or with a partner.

forward A player who tries to score on the opposing team's goal.

K point The distance to aim for when ski jumping, marked by the K line on the landing strip.

lava Hot, molten volcanic rock.

luge A type of sled with two runners, called steels, and a flat seat on which the rider lies down.

mogul A steep mound or ridge of snow on a ski slope.

muscles Tissue in the body that controls the movement of body parts.

penalty box A place where ice hockey players sit when taken out of play for breaking the rules.

professional A person who is paid to play a sport.

puck (ice hockey) A small, thick disc that players try to hit into the goals. Made of smooth rubber, it glides easily across the ice.

rink A frozen surface for ice hockey or skating, kept frozen by machines.

skateboard A board measuring about 29.5 inches (75cm) long and about 7.9 inches (20cm) wide with two wheels at each end.

skeleton A type of racing sled with two runners and a steel frame. Riders speed headfirst down a curving, icy track at up to 90 mph (145kph).

slalom A race course with obstacles that competitors must zigzag around.

surfboard A long, flat board about 9 feet (2.7m) long and 2 feet (0.6m) wide, used by surfers for riding waves in the ocean.

trail The path that a snowboarder or skier follows down a mountain, and that a cross-country skier follows through the countryside.

UFO Unidentified Flying Object.

Winter War A short war between the former Soviet Union and Finland (1939–1940).

WEB SITES
Snowboarding: www.abc-of-snowboarding.com
Skating: www.isu.org/
Ice hockey: www2.nhl.com/kids